Where are my shoes?

by Sue Bodman and Glen Franklin
illustrated by Ailie Busby

CAMBRIDGE
UNIVERSITY PRESS

UCL
Institute of Education

Taj went to the pool with Mum.

He took off his shoes
and went into the water.

'Oh, Taj,' said Mum. 'Look at this mess!'

It was time to go home.

Taj got out of the pool.

'Where are my shoes?' he said.

Taj looked for his shoes.

'Here they are,' he said.

Taj went to the beach with Mum.

He took off his shoes
and went on the sand.

'Look at this mess!' said Mum.

It was time to go home.

'Where are my shoes?' said Taj.

Mum came to help.

'Here they are,' said Taj.
'I can see my shoes.'

Taj went to the party with Mum.

10

He took off his shoes
and went on the bouncy castle.

Mum looked at all the shoes.

It was time to go home.

Taj looked for his shoes.

'Where are my shoes?' he said.

13

'Mum!' said Taj.

'Where is my shoe?'

14

Where are my shoes?  Sue Bodman and Glen Franklin

Teaching notes written by Sue Bodman and Glen Franklin

Using this book

Developing reading comprehension

Everywhere Taj and Mum go, he makes a mess and then can't find his shoes easily when it's time to·go home. He has to go home from a party with just one shoe.

The story uses familiar settings and events to ensure that the inferences required to gain precise meaning of the text are simple and straightforward.

Grammar and sentence structure

- Longer sentences (e.g. *'He took off his shoes and went into the water.'* p.3) are supported by shorter sentences (e.g. *'Look at this mess!'* p.5).
- Punctuation supports phrased and fluent reading.
- Direct speech uses natural language structures.

Word meaning and spelling

- Natural language structures: *'Here they are'*, *'Look at this mess'*.
- ...liar phonemes can be blended to check context ...od', 'pool', 'mess').

...ways that they can ...d their belongings, ...ld be the basis of a ...rota.

...different contexts. ...cal pairs amongst ...older children could ...airs or calculate pairs

Learning Outcomes

Children can:

- read aloud using the context, sentence structure and sight vocabulary to read with expression.
- attempt new words in more challenging texts using their phonic knowledge.
- comment on the events and characters in the story, making links to their own experience.

A guided reading lesson

Book Introduction

Give each child a book and read the title to them. Ask the children to look at the cover and suggest what is happening in the picture.

Orientation

Saying: *Taj is looking for his shoes. Have you ever lost your shoes?* Give a brief overview of the book, using the verb in the same form as it is in text: *Taj goes straight to play and doesn't put his shoes tidy. Then he has to look for them.*

Preparation

Page 2 and 3: Support the children with the story context. Say; *Taj went to the pool with Mum. But look what happened when he went into the water. Do you think Mum is happy? Why not? Let's find where Mum is talking. Yes, that's right, look for the speech marks. What does she say?* Observe as the children read the line *'Oh, Taj,' said Mum. 'Look at this mess!'* Were you right? What is she annoyed about? Yes, the mess. Let's check that word by saying it slowly. /m/ /e/ /ss/.